Answers to Your Social Security Questions That You Didn't Even Know to Ask

(2019 Edition)

CINDY LUNDQUIST

Answers To Your Social Security Questions That You Didn't Even Know To Ask (2019 Edition)

ISBN: 9781098569075

© 2019 Cindy Lundquist.

All rights reserved. No part of this book can be reproduced in any manner, except as permitted by U.S. copyright law, without the express written permission from the publisher.

The passage of the Social Security Act in 1935 marked a great advance in our concept of the means by which our citizens, through their Government, can provide against common economic risks.

- Harry S. Truman

Social Security is a social insurance program—it is not designed to be the same thing as a 401(k).

- Paul Krugman

ABOUT THE AUTHOR

Cindy Lundquist has worked as a Social Security, Medicare, and government benefits consultant for numerous government agencies for the last eighteen years. Her career began when she started working for the Social Security Administration in 1972. In 1999, the year she retired, she had risen to the position of executive assistant to the regional commissioner of the Social Security Administration in Atlanta, Georgia.

Since 1999 Lundquist has dedicated herself to providing education for government employees who are approaching retirement. Her sole desire is to enable them to make the right decisions about their benefits. Her government clients include the Department of Justice, Department of Defense, the US Marshals Service, Drug Enforcement Agency, and the Centers for Disease Control and Prevention.

Lundquist also serves as a consultant and lecturer for major American corporations. Her primary focus is on educating employees about how to maximize their Social Security benefits. Her corporate clients include Coca-Cola, Tropicana Products, Inc., Prudential, New York Life Insurance Company, and Cox Enterprises. Lundquist graduated from Georgia State University with a Bachelor of Arts degree in finance.

AUTHOR'S NOTE

The advice contained in this guide is meant to provide insight into Social Security, but it's important to understand that every person's situation is unique. Therefore, it's essential that you consult directly with experts in financial planning for retirement, and with tax attorneys and/or certified public accountants with expertise in retirement before making any decisions with regard to your Social Security and retirement cash flow strategies.

While we have made every effort to ensure that the information in this guide is reliable and accurate, ultimately the decisions you make about your Social Security benefits are your own. Neither the author nor the publisher can be held responsible for any difficulties, financial or otherwise, which may arise

FREE SOCIAL SECURITY NEWS & UPDATES

Go to https://cindylundquist.com to sign up for her FREE email newsletter that includes updates and information about Social Security, Medicare and other retirement benefits resources

CONTENTS

CHAPTER 1 - YOUR SOCIAL SECURITY BENEFITS 1

Retirement Benefits 2
What are retirement benefits? 2

Spousal Benefits 3
What is a spousal benefit? 3

Will a divorce impact my spousal benefits? 3

If I start my own Social Security retirement benefits, can I later file on the work record of my spouse or ex-spouse if half of their retirement benefits are worth more than my own retirement benefits? 4

If I'm divorced but want to remarry, will remarrying impact my Social Security benefits? 5

Can more than one ex-spouse draw on my record? 6

Does my former spouse have to be drawing Social Security benefits in order for me to draw spousal benefits as an ex-spouse? 6

As an ex-spouse drawing spousal benefits, do I have to worry about family maximums? 7

Can I draw spousal benefits if I'm under sixty-two? 8

Can I draw spousal benefits on my ex-spouse's record if I'm not sixty-two yet? 8

How do the new Social Security rules impact me? 8

Family Benefits 10
What is a family benefit? 10

Can my kids draw Social Security checks on my work record? 10

How much can my kids receive from my Social Security? 11

Survivor Benefits 11
What is a survivor benefit? 11

Can I take my survivor benefits and defer taking my retirement benefits? If so, what's the advantage? 12

My spouse is deceased. Will getting married again impact my Social Security benefits? 13

My spouse died a long time ago. Do survivor benefits still matter?...13

Can I collect survivor benefits if I got remarried and divorced?........14

I have been collecting Social Security benefits, and my spouse died. Can I switch to survivor benefits if those are higher?.................14

Can my kids draw survivor benefits?...14

Can I get survivor benefits before age sixty?..15

Disability Benefits 16

What's the most important thing I should know about Social Security disability benefits?...16

Do I have to pay into Social Security to get disability benefits?..........16

How is disability determined? 17

How are disability benefits calculated? 18

Do the same spousal or family eligibility rules apply for disability benefits as they do for drawing on a worker's retirement benefits?...18

Are survivor benefits the same when receiving disability benefits?....19

Is there anything that can reduce my disability benefits? 20

What should I do if my disability benefits are denied?.........................20

CHAPTER 2 - KEY SOCIAL SECURITY QUESTIONS 23

Do Social Security personnel give financial advice?.............................23

How much is the average monthly Social Security check?...................24

What are delayed retirement credits?...25

How do I maximize my Social Security benefits?..................................25

Can I collect Social Security and still work? 26

Can I collect Social Security if I've never worked?...............................28

Can I stop my Social Security benefits after I begin receiving them? 30

When do my Social Security benefits start?...30

When do I have to pay federal taxes on my Social Security income?. 32

Do sources of retirement income matter? 33

Should I worry about state income taxes on my Social Security?........34

Will Social Security be there for me? 35

What's the Windfall Elimination Provision? 38

What's a government pension offset? 38

My spouse receives Social Security retirement benefit checks. What happens when my spouse dies? Do I have to give back the check issued in the month of death? 39

CHAPTER 3 - TAKING EARLY BENEFITS 41

Why shouldn't I take my Social Security benefits early? 42

Does it ever make sense to take Social Security early? 43

Does taking a reduced Social Security benefit early also mean that my spouse's benefits will be reduced? 43

If I take spousal benefits early, are they reduced? 44

When does it make sense to take my spousal benefits early? 45

Is it true that if I take Social Security early I won't start losing money for seventeen years? 45

If we need the income, which spouse should take Social Security benefits early? 46

Does it make sense to use my investments to defer taking my Social Security benefits until age seventy? 46

CHAPTER 1
Your Social Security Benefits

Your Social Security benefits represent a valuable retirement investment. It pays to understand them before you claim any benefits you may be entitled to. For example, did you know you can collect survivor benefits and be remarried as long as the new marriage occurred after you turned sixty? Did you know that your kids might be eligible for Social Security checks equal to 75 percent of your full retirement benefits if you die? How about delayed retirement credits that can boost your retirement benefits by 76 percent between the age of sixty-two and seventy?

There's a lot to learn, so let's get started! The best place to begin is with a look at each of the benefit categories:

- Retirement
- Spousal
- Family
- Survivor
- Disability

We know you can find this basic benefit information on the Social Security Administration website. There are other sources on the Internet, some of which give you the wrong information, or just the basics rehashed from the SSA website. The beauty of this guide is that we have brought all the little details together in one place. Often obscure rules are included here, thereby giving you a leg up when it comes to understanding your Social Security benefits and the benefits your loved ones may be entitled to receive on your work record.

While your Social Security benefits might seem simple at first blush, they are more complicated than they seem. Maximizing benefits through informed decisions makes good financial sense. To maximize your benefits, you have to understand the basics first.

Retirement Benefits

What are retirement benefits?

Retirement benefits are the most basic and best understood in the Social Security program, but it's worth going over the basics anyway. You are eligible for your benefits if you meet the following requirements. You must be at least sixty-two years old or older. You have to have worked and paid Social Security taxes on your wages and/or your self-employment income for at least ten years, thereby accumulating forty credits of work. You are entitled to a monthly payment for the rest of your life.

If you take your retirement benefits early, they will be reduced forever. They will also be reduced for your survivors. We will discuss full retirement age and early benefits in the last chapter of this guide.

Other individuals can draw Social Security benefits based on your work record, but they have to meet certain eligibility requirements that will be explained in the following sections.

Spousal Benefits

What is a spousal benefit?

If you have been married for one year or more, you are potentially entitled to draw spousal benefits when you reach age sixty-two or more. Your spouse must be receiving Social Security benefits. Your retirement benefits must be less than 50 percent of your spouse's full retirement benefits. If your retirement benefits are worth more, you would get your retirement benefits instead of spousal benefits. Maximum spousal benefits are equal to 50 percent of your spouse's retirement benefits.

Will a divorce impact my spousal benefits?

Many people don't think about Social Security when it comes to divorce, but it does matter. As an ex-spouse, you may be entitled to spousal benefits on your former spouse's record if you've been married for at least ten years. If you're close to your tenth wedding anniversary and thinking about getting a divorce, wait to file for divorce until after your tenth wedding anniversary passes. Your retirement benefits must be less than 50 percent of your ex-spouse's retirement benefits for this strategy to make sense. If your retirement benefits are worth more, you would get your retirement benefits instead of ex-spousal benefits.

Spousal benefits are equal to 50 percent of your ex-spouse's retirement benefits at his or her full retirement age if you wait until full retirement age to collect them. In other words, if your ex-spouse collects reduced retirement benefits before reaching full retirement age, you won't be penalized for it. You'll still get the full 50 percent of his or her retirement benefits if you wait until you reach full retirement age before you begin receiving your monthly spousal benefit checks.

If I start my own Social Security retirement benefits, can I later file on the work record of my spouse or ex-spouse if half of their retirement benefits are worth more than my own retirement benefits?

In some cases, you can do so. For example, let's say you were single and you filed for your retirement benefits at your full retirement age of sixty-six. Hypothetically, we'll assume your monthly check is $1,000. Now let's assume you got married and your spouse was also at full retirement age and collecting a retirement benefit of $2,250 per month. Remember that maximum spousal benefits at your full retirement age are worth half of your spouse's full retirement benefits, so half of $2,250 equals $1,125. In this case, your spousal benefits would be worth more than your own retirement benefits. You must be married for one year to collect spousal benefits. You'd need to contact the Social Security Administration to initiate the change to the higher benefit amount after your first wedding anniversary.

If you were already married and you waited until your full retirement age to file for your retirement benefits, you would receive spousal benefits if those benefits were worth more than your retirement benefits.

The answer to the question changes when you take your retirement benefits early. Let's say your unreduced benefit is $1,000 at full retirement age, but you start receiving your checks at sixty-two. The amount of the reduction would be approximately 25 percent if your full retirement age is sixty-six. Your monthly check would go down to $750 if you began your retirement benefits at sixty-two. If your spouse's retirement benefit is $1,800, 50 percent of that amount equals $900. You might assume that your check will increase to $900 rather than $750 if you took spousal benefits. Unfortunately, the $250 reduction is still imposed. In this example, $900 minus $250 results in a smaller $650 check for spousal benefits. Therefore, you would continue to receive your retirement benefits.

As you can see, sorting through Social Security benefits can get complicated! You must be proactive and contact the Social Security Administration to see if you are entitled to an increased benefit.

If I'm divorced but want to remarry, will remarrying impact my Social Security benefits?

When you remarry, you lose eligibility for spousal benefits on your ex-spouse's work record. If you're already collecting them, they'll cease when you get remarried. You will also lose eligibility for survivor benefits on your deceased ex-spouse's record if you remarry prior to age sixty. Should the subsequent marriage terminate you would again have potential eligibility.

In some cases, it makes sense to not get remarried. For example, if you've never worked and your ex-spouse was a very high earner, your spousal or survivor benefits could be substantial. The spousal or survivor benefits you would be eligible for under your new spouse's record could be substantially less if you remarry. Of course, the opposite could be true, depending on the financial status of your new spouse. Keep that in mind when making decisions about remarrying, especially if you've never worked and paid into Social Security.

Can more than one ex-spouse draw on my record?

If you have more than one ex-spouse who is eligible for spousal benefits on your work record, each can draw benefits. This will not impact the amount of your retirement benefits. Each of your ex-spouses will have to have been married to you for ten years or more. They couldn't have remarried and still be married, and they would have to be sixty-two or older. If you're currently married, your current spouse could also collect spousal benefits as long as the eligibility requirements are met.

As an ex-spouse receiving spousal benefits on your ex-spouse's work record, it doesn't matter how many times your ex-spouse gets married and divorced. The ex-spouse's marital status doesn't impact you at all.

Does my former spouse have to be drawing Social Security benefits in order for me to draw spousal benefits as an ex-spouse?

If you were applying for spousal benefits as a current spouse, your spouse would have to be drawing retirement benefits for you to be eligible. But as an ex-spouse your former spouse only has to be sixty-two. He or she doesn't have to be drawing retirement benefits. In fact, your ex-spouse can still be working. You can begin taking reduced spousal benefits at sixty-two as long as you were married to your ex-spouse for ten years or more. If your ex-spouse isn't taking benefits, you have to have been divorced for at least two years for you to draw spousal benefits on your ex-spouse's work record. If your retirement benefits exceed 50 percent of the full retirement benefits of your ex-spouse, you would not be eligible for spousal benefits as an ex-spouse. You would receive your retirement benefits instead.

Don't forget that earnings limits apply when you take reduced spousal benefits before you reach full retirement age. You could only earn $17,640 in 2019 before the Social Security Administration would begin to withhold benefits if you exceeded the limit. We'll discuss the earnings limit in more detail later.

Taking your benefits early may not be the right decision, depending on your employment situation. If you are earning good money and don't mind working, it makes better sense to stay in the workforce and grow your retirement benefits by waiting until full retirement age to begin receiving your monthly checks, or by waiting until age seventy to maximize your retirement benefits through the accumulation of delayed retirement credits.

As an ex-spouse drawing spousal benefits, do I have to worry about family maximums?

The Social Security Administration has what's known as a family maximum. In other words, the SSA won't pay out an unlimited amount in benefits to various members of a family who are drawing benefits on a worker's record.

In most cases, you will be drawing retirement benefits, not spousal benefits as an ex-spouse. If you are eligible for spousal benefits as an ex-spouse the following scenario could sometimes apply. Your ex-spouse may have a spouse drawing spousal benefits on his or her work record. If your ex-spouse's current spouse is under sixty-two and caring for children under age sixteen, or who were disabled prior to reaching age twenty-two, the children may also be drawing on your ex-spouse's record. When multiple family members draw on one record, a family maximum of between 150 to 180 percent of the worker's retirement benefits applies. The great news for you as an ex-spouse is that the family maximum does not apply to you! Your benefits will not be reduced because of the family maximum.

Can I draw spousal benefits if I'm under sixty-two?

The answer is yes, but you and your spouse have to meet certain eligibility requirements. Your spouse must be sixty-two and drawing Social Security retirement benefits, or your spouse must be receiving Social Security disability benefits. You have to be caring for children under age sixteen, or for a child that became disabled before age twenty-two. The children can be the result of the marriage, adopted, or the stepchildren of you or your spouse. A child born out of wedlock is also eligible.

Your benefit amount would be equal to 50 percent of your spouse's retirement benefits at full retirement age. You would stop receiving benefits when the youngest child reaches age sixteen. Your check wouldn't stop if you're caring for a child who was disabled before the age of twenty-two. No duration of marriage rule applies to you in this case. You can start collecting your checks after you apply for them.

Can I draw spousal benefits on my ex-spouse's record if I'm not sixty-two yet?

Unfortunately, the answer is no. You must be sixty-two even if you are caring for a child of your ex-spouse who is younger than sixteen, or if you are taking care of your ex-spouse's child who became disabled prior to turning twenty-two. If your ex-spouse dies and you are caring for his or her young or disabled children, you would potentially be eligible for a mother or father's benefit.

How do the new Social Security rules impact me?

In November 2015, some key rules in the Social Security program were changed in provisions embedded in the Bipartisan Budget Act. The new rules essentially make spousal benefits less important.

Here's why.

Prior to the big changes, you could file for spousal benefits on your spouse's Social Security record when you reached full retirement age, and then ask for a restricted application. The application would allow you to defer taking your retirement benefits in favor of your spousal benefits. This allowed you to take advantage of delayed retirement credits of 8 percent per year until age seventy while you were also drawing spousal benefits equal to 50 percent of your spouse's retirement benefits. We'll discuss delayed retirement credits in more detail later. Suffice it to say here that Congress got wise to this supposed loophole in spousal benefits after the alleged double-dipping strategy hit the news. The outcry led to legislative action that resulted in the changes that closed the loophole.

Now you can't file an application to restrict your benefits. The Social Security Administration will "deem" you, whereby you'll get whichever benefit is greater, either your spousal benefits or your retirement benefits. In most cases, your retirement benefits will exceed your spousal benefits, so spousal benefits essentially become moot for most of us. Of course, if you've never worked and paid into Social Security, spousal benefits as a current spouse or as an ex-spouse are very important if you meet the eligibility requirements.

However, if you were born in 1953 or earlier you can still file an application to restrict your benefits to spousal benefits while deferring your retirement benefits to grow them until age seventy. This is the case even if your retirement benefits exceed your spousal benefits. If you were born in 1954 or later, you have to take the higher of the two benefits.

The end result of the changes is that those of us born in 1954 or after can't defer our retirement benefits while taking spousal benefits.

That's a loss of 24 percent in delayed retirement credits for those of us whose full retirement age is sixty-seven. Some sources estimate that the loss amounts to as much as $50,000 per couple in some instances!

Family Benefits

What is a family benefit?

A family benefit is a monthly Social Security check for a family member based on your work record. Many people don't know about family benefits. As a result, they sometimes lose benefits they could otherwise have received if they'd only known they were eligible for them.

Can my kids draw Social Security checks on my work record?

Children can draw benefits on your work record when you begin receiving your retirement benefits. They can receive a check if they're under the age of eighteen. If they are still in high school at age eighteen, checks will continue until they graduate, or until they turn nineteen, whichever occurs first. Children can draw benefits up to age eighteen even if they are not in high school. You and the kids can begin receiving checks as soon as your application goes through. If a child drawing benefits gets married, the benefits will cease. Benefits also cease on the month before the child's eighteenth birthday unless they are still in high school or disabled.

How much can my kids receive from my Social Security?

Regardless of whether you start your retirement checks before your full retirement age, each child could get a monthly check equal to 50 percent of your full retirement benefits. There is a limit regarding how much Social Security will pay in family benefits. The limit is set at between 150 to 180 percent of you or your spouse's retirement benefits at full retirement age. Typically, the total is about 170 percent of the worker's retirement benefit at full retirement age. Combined family benefits can amount to several thousand dollars. They are definitely worth factoring into your retirement and financial planning, if you meet the necessary eligibility criteria.

Survivor Benefits

What is a survivor benefit?

Simply put, survivor benefits are paid to those who are eligible for them based on your work record prior to your death. The more you pay into Social Security, the more valuable your survivor benefits will be to your loved ones. That is one reason why we don't recommend taking your retirement benefits early. Doing so reduces your survivor benefits. Spouses, ex-spouses, and family members may be eligible for survivor benefits.

How much is my survivor benefit?

Your survivor benefit depends on the earnings history of your deceased spouse or ex-spouse. You qualify for survivor benefits as a spouse if you've been married for at least nine months prior to your spouse's death, or if you were married to your ex-spouse for ten years or more. The more your deceased spouse or ex-spouse earned, the higher your benefit will be.

If you wait until full retirement age to collect your survivor benefits, you will receive 100 percent of your deceased spouse's full retirement benefits. Your survivor benefits will be reduced if you take them early. If you take them at age sixty, your survivor benefits will be equal to 71.5 percent of your deceased spouse's retirement benefits at full retirement age. If you're disabled, you can take reduced survivor benefits at age 50 (71.5 percent of your deceased spouse's benefits at full retirement age).

Can I take my survivor benefits and defer taking my retirement benefits? If so, what's the advantage?

Survivor benefits are separate from your retirement benefits. In other words, if you take survivor benefits early it doesn't mean your retirement benefits will be reduced too. If you take survivor benefits, you can defer taking your retirement benefits. This will allow you to grow your retirement benefits until age seventy. If your survivor benefits still exceeded your retirement benefits when you reached age seventy, you'd stick with the survivor benefits. If your retirement benefits are worth more than your survivor benefits, you'd switch over to your retirement benefits.

Here's another option to consider for survivors who have worked enough to get their own retirement check, but the check is much smaller than a survivor benefit. If your survivor benefits will always be more than your retirement benefits, even with the extra credits you could receive for waiting until age seventy to collect, you could start your own reduced retirement benefits at age sixty-two, and then switch to the deceased worker's record at full retirement age. This would allow you to maximize your survivor benefit.

My spouse is deceased. Will getting married again impact my Social Security benefits?

Many people overlook survivor benefits. These benefits can be very valuable, especially if you are or were a low earner. Survivor benefits can exceed your retirement benefits. You will lose the survivor benefits on the record of the deceased spouse if you remarry prior to age sixty. If you remarry before age sixty, but that subsequent marriage terminates, you will again be eligible for survivor benefits. If you wait to remarry at age sixty or thereafter, you will retain the survivor benefits on the record of the deceased spouse. You will have to have been married for at least nine months to do so.

After you've been married to your new spouse for at least nine months, you'll qualify for survivor benefits on his or her record. If your new spouse dies and his or her survivor benefits are higher than those of your first spouse, you could apply for them instead. If you wait until reaching full retirement age, your survivor benefits will equal 100 percent of the higher of either deceased spouse's full retirement benefits.

My spouse died a long time ago. Do survivor benefits still matter?

Many people make the mistake of dismissing survivor benefits, especially if the spouse died a long time ago and never earned much money. It's worth noting that the benefit amounts will have continued to grow after death because of cost-of-living adjustments made to keep up with inflation. If you are a low earner, your survivor benefits could exceed your retirement benefits. You'd receive survivor benefits instead of your retirement benefits.

Your reduced survivor benefits of 71.5 percent of your deceased spouse's full retirement benefits at age sixty could exceed your retirement benefits, which means that you could begin collecting Social Security at age sixty instead of at age sixty-two or later.

Can I collect survivor benefits if I got remarried and divorced?

You can have been married and divorced multiple times. You can't be currently married prior to age sixty and collect survivor benefits on your deceased spouse or spouses.

If you divorced your deceased spouse, got remarried, and then your second spouse died, you'd draw survivor benefits on the higher of the two records. You'd have to have been married for ten years or more to the first spouse. You would only have to have been married to your second spouse for nine months at the time of death.

I have been collecting Social Security benefits, and my spouse died. Can I switch to survivor benefits if those are higher?

Many people don't even consider that option because they don't know about it. If your current retirement benefits are less than your survivor benefits, you would switch to survivor benefits.

Can my kids draw survivor benefits?

Children below age eighteen can draw survivor benefits, and teens eighteen years old and still in high school can also draw survivor benefits. If a child was disabled prior to turning age twenty-two, he or she is eligible for survivor benefits. The benefit amount is 75 percent of the deceased worker's full retirement benefits.

Can I get survivor benefits before age sixty?

If you are disabled, you can begin drawing reduced survivor benefits as early as age fifty.

You are eligible for survivor benefits prior to age sixty if you are caring for a child of your deceased spouse who is younger than sixteen, or if you are taking care of a child of your deceased spouse who became disabled prior to turning twenty-two. Bear in mind once again that survivor benefits are reduced forever if your spouse takes retirement benefits early. If a child gets married, benefits cease.

Disability Benefits

Disability benefits are in a separate class. They are not like retirement, spousal, family, or survivor benefits. Let's take a close look at disability benefits. Knowing the rules about Social Security disability benefits could make a big difference in the quality of life if you or a loved one is disabled.

What's the most important thing I should know about Social Security disability benefits?

If you can work in any capacity, you are not entitled to disability benefits from Social Security. If you want to apply for disability benefits, you have to prove that you are unable to work due to a physical or mental condition that is expected to last for twelve months or longer, or that will lead to your death. You have to be an American citizen, or a legal alien, and you have to be under full retirement age if you're an adult.

Do I have to pay into Social Security to get disability benefits?

As with any other benefit from Social Security, you have to pay into the program to qualify. But there are extra rules when it comes to disability benefits.

You have to have paid into Social Security for a total of forty quarters. And here's the extra hurdle. You have to have a work record of twenty quarters for at least five years going back ten years prior to the date of your disability. If you retire early, say at age fifty, and you are disabled at sixty-one, you won't qualify for disability benefits because you wouldn't have worked at least twenty quarters in the last ten years prior to your disability. It won't matter if you've paid into the program for forty quarters during your working life. Of course, if you did pay into Social Security for forty quarters prior to retiring at age fifty, you would qualify for retirement benefits. You could take reduced retirement benefits at age sixty-two.

The exception with regard to the twenty quarters paid in within the last ten years prior to your disability is if you are disabled before you turn thirty-one. In that case, you have to have half the quarters prior to your disability. For example, if you were disabled at twenty-nine, you'd need to have at least eighteen quarters between the age of twenty-one and twenty-nine, or two credits per year for nine years. If you were disabled around the time of your twenty-first birthday, you would need at least six quarters to qualify.

If you worked a federal, state, local government, or other job (like a teacher in some districts) and you did not pay into Social Security, you would not be eligible for disability benefits. You would have to meet the eligibility requirements outlined above in order to qualify for disability benefits.

How is disability determined?

Obviously, you'll need to provide a written assessment from a medical professional about your physical or mental status. Your application for disability benefits is then sent to a special state-run office. An official in that office will review your medical records and other documentation, and then forward an approval or denial recommendation to the Social Security Administration. If it is determined that you can work in any capacity based on your age, education, and previous employment history, you will not be eligible for disability benefits.

If you are approved for disability benefits, your case will be reviewed every one to seven years to ensure that your condition has not improved. If it has and it's determined that you can work, your benefits will stop. If your condition is likely to be permanent, you'll still be reviewed once every seven years or so.

How are disability benefits calculated?

The benefit amount is based on your earnings history, just like your retirement benefits. The more you pay into the Social Security program, the higher your monthly checks will be. Disability benefits are paid based on the retirement benefit you would have received if you were at full retirement age when you became disabled. Think of it like you got your full retirement benefits at the time you were disabled.

Do the same spousal or family eligibility rules apply for disability benefits as they do for drawing on a worker's retirement benefits?

The rules are the same. For a current spouse, you have to be married for one year or more and be sixty-two or older. Your retirement benefits have to be worth less than 50 percent of the disabled spouse's disability benefits. The same goes for you as an ex-spouse, except you'll have to have been married for ten years, and you'd have to be currently unmarried.

Children up to age nineteen who are still in high school can receive a check. Children who are under age eighteen don't need to be in high school to receive a check. If you are under sixty-two and are caring for minor children under sixteen, or if you're caring for disabled children who were disabled before the age of twenty-two, you can receive a check. Combined checks can make a big financial difference in the lives of the disabled and their families.

Benefit amounts for family members are different under disability. The family maximum is up to 150 percent of your disability benefits. Family maximums for other benefits can go up to 180 percent of the worker's full retirement benefits. The calculation for determining the maximum for family members is different from retirement and survivor benefits. The formula used to determine family maximum benefits in disability cases produces a smaller payment, and in some cases the children will not receive any payment. If minor and disabled children qualify for payments, each may receive up to 50 percent of your disability benefits. Your spouse or ex-spouse can receive up to 50 percent of your disability benefits. Ex-spouses aren't subject to the family maximum. Family members drawing on your record as a disabled person are each subject to the earnings limit, which was $17,640 in 2019.

Are survivor benefits the same when receiving disability benefits?

Survivor benefit amounts are the same when it comes to disability cases. However, if you are disabled, you can claim your reduced survivor benefits at age fifty, as opposed to age sixty if you are not disabled. The reduced benefit amount at fifty would be 71.5 percent of your deceased spouse's full retirement benefits. If you waited until reaching full retirement age, your survivor benefit would be equal to 100 percent of your deceased spouse's full retirement benefits.

If your existing disability benefits are worth more than your survivor benefits, you would not be eligible for survivor benefits. If your survivor benefits are worth more than your disability benefits, your disability benefits would be increased to include-survivor benefits.

Is there anything that can reduce my disability benefits?

If you were injured on the job and qualified for workman's compensation, a family cannot receive benefits worth more than 80 percent of the disabled worker's previous wages. Both the Social Security disability and worker's compensation payments are counted against that 80 percent figure. The benefit reductions apply in most states, though there are a few states that will reduce your workman's compensation payments instead of your disability benefits.

If you did pay into Social Security for forty quarters, you may be eligible for disability benefits even if you were a public servant working in a position that didn't pay into Social Security. Remember, you must have recent work where you paid Social Security taxes five out of the last ten years before you became disabled. However, your Social Security disability benefits would be reduced through what is known as the Windfall Elimination Provision. The reduction is typically 50 percent of the disability benefit amount. Please see the next chapter for more information on the Windfall Elimination Provision.

What should I do if my disability benefits are denied?

If you are turned down for disability benefits and you believe you are entitled to them, file an appeal for reconsideration within sixty days of the denial. If you miss the sixty-day deadline, you'll have to file a new application.

Reconsideration is excluded in the following locations: Alabama, Alaska, Colorado, Louisiana, Missouri, Michigan, New York, Pennsylvania, and North and West Los Angeles. You can still appeal the denial, but you'll have to go before an administrative law judge.

If your petition for reconsideration is denied, or you live in a state where reconsideration isn't done, you can appeal and get the case heard by an administrative law judge. We recommend hiring an attorney, preferably one who has worked for the Social Security Administration, or who has a proven track record in disability cases. Expect it to take a year or two to get the case heard. If approved on appeal, the benefits are payable retroactively back to when you first applied, provided that the appeals process was not dropped for any reason. If the judge rules against you, you can go before the Appeals Council to have your case heard.

If the Appeals Council rules against you, you can go to federal court. Hardly anyone ever does this because of the expensive legal fees.

CHAPTER 2
Key Social Security Questions

One of the biggest mistakes people make when it comes to claiming their Social Security benefits is going into the process without enough knowledge. As we mentioned, some aspects of Social Security are complicated. Questions that can boost benefits for you and your loved ones are often overlooked. The following chapter will provide you with a number of questions that could apply to your circumstances. We think some of the answers may surprise you.

Do Social Security personnel give financial advice?

Social Security personnel are not allowed to give you financial advice. They are there to answer your questions and to assist you with the claiming process. If you don't know which questions to ask, you may not get all the information you need to make the right decisions about your Social Security benefits. We recommend that you consider seeking advice from professionals such as licensed certified financial planners or wealth managers that specialize in retirement benefits and investing. Contacting a certified public accountant with retirement expertise is also recommended, particularly when it comes to tax minimization on retirement income, including income from Social Security benefits.

How much is the average monthly Social Security check?

The average monthly Social Security check for an individual in 2019 is $1,461. The amount of your benefits is based on your highest earnings over a period of thirty-five years. If you work fewer than thirty-five years, your benefits will be based on your earnings history during those years. If you work longer than thirty-five years, you can boost your benefits because only the highest thirty-five years of earnings will be counted. Thus, you can effectively bump lower earnings years out of the calculation if your income is higher than it was in previous years.

After age sixty, the progressive formula used in assigning benefits no longer applies. That means that working after age sixty gives you an extra bonus in terms of nudging low earnings years out of your thirty-five-year earnings history. If you remain gainfully employed until age seventy, chances are you'll not only banish the lowest of earnings years from your work record, you will also grow your retirement benefits by 8 percent per year through delayed retirement credits.

In 2019, the maximum taxable annual earnings for Social Security hit $132,900. If you paid the maximum for the full highest thirty-five years of your work history that are used to calculate your retirement benefits (assuming you worked for thirty-five years or more), you would reach the maximum monthly Social Security benefit. In 2019, that benefit is $2,876.

It's worth pointing out that a married couple who were both high earners for most of their working lives can expect to receive as much as $500,000 each in Social Security benefits if they both live long and prosper! Before you pop the champagne cork it's also worth noting that numerous sources say the combined healthcare costs for a retired couple will exceed $250,000 even with Medicare, assuming one or both of the spouses live into their late eighties or early nineties.

What are delayed retirement credits?

We've mentioned delayed retirement credits in earlier pages. Let's just sum up here. After you reach full retirement age, you can increase your Social Security by 8 percent per year until age seventy. In other words, you can rack up valuable credit on your benefits by not taking them until you reach age seventy. The benefit increase would be 32 percent if your full retirement age is sixty-six. Considering that almost half of Americans rely on Social Security for 50 percent of their retirement income, that 32 percent increase through delayed retirement credits can make a big difference in the quality of life during retirement.

If you don't take reduced Social Security benefits at sixty-two and you take full advantage of delayed retirement credits, your retirement benefits will increase by 76 percent between the age of sixty-two and seventy if your full retirement age is sixty-six. Think about that the next time you yearn to take your retirement benefits at age sixty-two. For the sake of simplicity, let's say your reduced monthly retirement benefit at sixty-two was $1,000. That amount would go up to $1,760 at age seventy, or a difference of $760 per month. That's the equivalent of $9,120 per year. If you live to age eighty, that's a whopping $91,200 for the ten-year period!

How do I maximize my Social Security benefits?

You can boost your benefits by waiting until your full retirement age to collect them. If you wait until age seventy, you'll increase your benefits through delayed retirement credits. If you keep working beyond your full retirement age and delay collecting your benefits, you'll be paying into the program, thereby benefiting from the possibility of bumping low earnings years from your work history. Your earnings history is used to calculate your benefit amount. Also, your benefits are increased through cost-of-living adjustments to keep up with inflation. These are all ways to maximize your Social Security.

Can I collect Social Security and still work?

If you have reached full retirement age, you can earn as much as you like, but if you are between sixty-two and full retirement age you can't exceed the earnings limit. The earnings limit in 2019 was $17,640. If you and your spouse are drawing benefits on your own work records, then you can each earn up to $17,640 without losing any of your benefits. The earnings limit is adjusted for inflation every year, which means the limit typically increases a little every year.

The Social Security Administration withholds one dollar of your benefits for every two dollars you earn over the limit. In the year you reach full retirement age, your earnings threshold increases to $46,920 up to the month you reach full retirement age. If you exceed the earnings limit in this time period, the Social Security Administration will withhold one dollar for every three dollars from your benefits. When you reach your full retirement age, you can earn as much as you want and still draw your checks.

Wages and self-employment income are counted in the earnings limit. Income from dividend-paying stocks, and IRA and 401(k) withdrawals doesn't impact the earnings limit. That means an excellent retirement planning strategy entails building up investment income sources that aren't counted in the earnings limit. Doing so could allow you to take reduced benefits early and still enjoy good retirement cash flow. Incidentally, if you're wondering how the SSA will know if you exceed the earnings limit, you should be aware that the IRS shares information with the SSA.

It's also worth noting that earnings limits apply to each family member drawing on your work record. Benefits will be held back for each individual recipient if he or she exceeds the earnings limit. So, if you're under sixty-two and receiving Social Security checks based on your spouse's work record, you could lose benefits if you got a job that paid well.

Many retirees take Social Security at sixty-two and they work part-time or full-time jobs that pay at or just above the earnings limit. While we don't recommend taking your benefits early, doing so can work in your favor. You can get income from your reduced retirement benefits and earn up to the earnings limit. The wages plus the retirement benefits can give you and your spouse a modest income while allowing you to retire early, or at least to go part-time. It also doesn't matter much if you go a little over the earnings limit because the dollar amount of the benefits that will be taken back would be low.

However, if you know you're going to earn a substantial amount over the earnings limit, we strongly recommend that you contact the Social Security Administration to adjust your payments, thereby avoiding overpayments in your benefits for that year. Let's say you suddenly get a really great job, and you decide you want to go for it but are collecting reduced Social Security benefits because you took them early. The SSA will suspend your benefit payments. That can help boost the value of your reduced benefits when benefits are reinstated later. If you keep working until you're seventy, you will benefit from delayed retirement credits as well.

Periodically obtain your Social Security statement from the Social Security Administration so you know what benefit amounts you are eligible to receive. The easiest way to go is to set up an account on the Social Security website (www.ssa.gov). The SSA has discontinued their automatic mailing of statements. It's up to you to access your most recent statement prior to making any decisions about your benefits. The SSA website has a benefit calculator to help you understand your benefit projections.

Your projected retirement benefit amounts will change over time. The calculations you see on your statement reflect your current earnings history. You will see what you'll get at sixty-two if you take early benefits, what you'll get at full retirement age, and what you'll receive if you wait until age seventy to start collecting your monthly check. If your income drops over time, those benefits will be lower. If your income increases over time, those benefits will be higher.

Many people make the mistake of thinking their benefits are static based on their most recent statement. If you don't check your statement just before you plan to collect benefits, you may be in for an unpleasant surprise. You can apply for benefits online, but we recommend that you make an appointment at your local Social Security office to ask questions before you claim your benefits.

Can I collect Social Security if I've never worked?

You can only collect Social Security if you've worked at least forty quarters and paid into the program. That's why working off the books is such a bad idea. If you have never married and never paid into Social Security, it also means you don't get Medicare Part A (hospitalization) for free. If you've never worked and paid into Social Security, you are not eligible for disability benefits if you become disabled.

Let's assume you never married, but you did work a little and paid into Social Security for twenty-nine or fewer quarters. If that's the case, you can buy Medicare Part A coverage. In 2019, the monthly premium is $437 in this case. If you paid into Social Security for thirty to thirty-nine quarters, the monthly premium for Medicare Part A in 2019 is $240.

If you've never paid into Social Security, or if you've only paid in a little, getting married to someone who has paid into the program for forty quarters or more could substantially improve your quality of life in retirement. The benefit for free Medicare Part A coverage was equal to $5,244 in 2019. And that doesn't even take into account the value of spousal and survivor benefits if you've never worked and paid into Social Security.

Now let's assume you are married, or you are divorced but not remarried. The good news is that you may be eligible for spousal benefits if you've been married for at least one year. You may be eligible for spousal benefits as an ex-spouse if you were married for ten years prior to the divorce. Plus, you may also qualify for Medicare Part A if you meet the eligibility requirements as a spouse or as an ex-spouse. At full retirement age, spousal benefits are 50 percent of your spouse or ex-spouse's full retirement benefits. Current and ex-spouses each can draw on the worker's Social Security work record. You can receive reduced spousal benefits if you begin taking them at sixty-two.

You are eligible for survivor benefits if your spouse dies and you have been married for at least nine months. You must be unmarried unless your current marriage occurred when you are 60 or older. At your full retirement age, survivor benefits are equal to 100 percent of your deceased spouse's full retirement benefits. You can begin drawing a reduced survivor benefit at age sixty. The benefit at age sixty is equal to 71.5 percent of your deceased spouse's full retirement benefit. You can also qualify for free or reduced-cost Medicare Part A when you reach the age of sixty-five.

If you were married for ten years and then divorced and you are currently unmarried or your current marriage occurred when you are 60 or older, you would also qualify for survivor benefits as an ex-spouse. You'd also be eligible for Medicare Part A.

Can I stop my Social Security benefits after I begin receiving them?

You have the chance to stop (withdraw) your Social Security benefits within one year of starting to receive them. Even waiting a day beyond one year will eliminate the option to withdraw. If you withdraw, you will have to repay all benefits received before the one-year deadline. No interest charges apply.

After you reach full retirement age, you can suspend your benefits. You do not have to repay the benefits you received. The beauty of suspending is that if you took reduced benefits early, you can stop them and take advantage of delayed retirement credits of 8 percent per year until age seventy. This can help make up for the benefit reduction that occurred when you took your benefits early. Suspending your benefits will mean that any other benefits paid out on your work record will also stop. This includes spousal and family benefits.

When do my Social Security benefits start?

Benefits start in the first month you file an application for benefits.

What are back Social Security benefits?

In some cases, you are entitled to receive payments you were owed but didn't collect yet. For example, let's say you waited almost a year after reaching your full retirement age to file an application for benefits. The Social Security Administration will pay you benefits going back six months. The SSA will only pay back benefits for six months. Still, it's worth knowing about this because every Social Security check counts. If you know you're going to start collecting as soon as you reach full retirement age, it's best to apply no more than three months prior to that date.

Back benefits are not payable if you begin receiving your retirement checks before full retirement. Reduced benefits are payable beginning the month you file your application to receive the checks.

If you're entitled to back benefits, you don't have to get a retroactive check. Instead, you can ask the SSA to add six months of delayed retirement credits toward future benefits (provided you were in fact owed six months). In other words, you'll build your benefit value if you ask for a credit instead of a retroactive check.

If your spouse dies and you are eligible for survivor benefits and you want to begin collecting them, it's important to apply right away, or at least within six months of your spouse's death if you are at full retirement age at the time of his or her death. Many grieving spouses don't file for their survivor benefits in a timely fashion. Thus, they lose out on benefits they could otherwise have collected. Remember, the SSA will only pay back benefits for six months if you are at full retirement age, and the SSA will pay no back benefits if you are filing for reduced survivor benefits. Also, remember that collecting survivor benefits, or any other Social Security benefit, only makes sense if you're not working, or you're not going to greatly exceed the earnings limit if you do work.

There is a slight difference when it comes to Social Security disability benefits. When your application for disability benefits is approved, there is a five-month waiting period before you begin collecting your monthly checks. Back benefits go back to the time you were disabled and filed for benefits, less the five-month waiting period. For example, if you became disabled, filed twelve months later, and were approved immediately, you would receive seven months of back disability benefits.

When do I have to pay federal taxes on my Social Security income?

Not all of your Social Security income is subject to federal tax. In fact, you might not have to pay any taxes on benefits, depending on your income and on the source of your income.

In 2019, if you filed an individual tax return, and your modified adjusted gross income, or MAGI, was less than $25,000, you wouldn't have paid any federal taxes on your Social Security income. If you earned between $25,000 and $34,000, 50 percent of your Social Security income was subject to federal taxes. If you earned more than that, then 85 percent of your Social Security income was taxed at the federal rate applicable to your federal income tax bracket.

If you filed a joint tax return, either in a traditional or in a same-sex marriage, 50 percent of Social Security income was taxed at the federal level if your modified adjusted gross income was between $32,000 and $44,000. If you both earned more than that, then 85 percent of your Social Security income was subject to federal taxes.

Do sources of retirement income matter?

Wages, interest, non-qualified dividends, and pension income are all figured into your modified adjusted gross income, which in turn is used to determine whether you cross the federal tax threshold on Social Security benefit income. These sources of income, plus the taxable portion of your Social Security benefits, are taxed as ordinary income. In other words, they'll be treated just like wages. Your federal tax liability depends on which tax bracket you're in.

It's important to note that qualified dividends are not taxed in the lowest two tax brackets, and they are taxed as long-term capital gains in higher brackets. Long-term capital gains are usually taxed at a lower rate than ordinary income. Most of the dividends you'll receive from big companies like Ford and Coca-Cola are qualified dividends. Income from these dividends will not count toward your modified adjusted gross income, which in turn won't be factored into the federal tax threshold on Social Security income.

Although we aren't certified financial planners, we strongly recommend structuring some or most of your retirement investments to take full advantage of the tax break you get from qualified dividends. Talk with your financial advisor about these investments for your retirement portfolio. It's possible for you to pay little or no tax on your Social Security and your investment income!

Many retirees work. As noted, wages are taxed as ordinary income and thereby impact on whether (and how much) Social Security income is taxed. Usually, these same retirees have fixed income accounts that generate interest income or income from non-qualified dividends. Both are taxed at your marginal income tax rate, just like wages. The tax bite from federal and state taxes can put a serious dent in your Social Security and retirement investment income. Tax minimization through strategic investing can maximize your Social Security benefits.

Should I worry about state income taxes on my Social Security?

Some states do tax Social Security benefit income. These income Colorado, Connecticut, Kansas, Minnesota, Missouri, Montana, Nebraska, New Mexico, North Dakota, Rhode Island, Utah, Vermont, and West Virginia. Minimizing tax liabilities should be a key part of your Social Security strategy. If you live in one of these states, give some thought to relocating to a state that doesn't tax your Social Security income. If you relocate to a state with lower state and property taxes, you'll have more of your Social Security benefits to spend during your retirement.

Does every state tax pensions?

As mentioned earlier, pensions are considered ordinary income in the eyes of the IRS. So is Social Security income above the federal tax threshold. Adding state tax liabilities to your pension on top of taxes on Social Security income is a poor retirement strategy. If you are lucky enough to have a pension, relocating to a state that doesn't tax Social Security or pensions is a sound retirement strategy.

Sadly, only twelve states don't tax Social Security or pensions. These include Alabama, Alaska, Florida, Mississippi, Nevada, New Hampshire, Pennsylvania, South Dakota, Tennessee, Texas, Washington, and Wyoming. That doesn't mean you're totally out of luck if you don't want to move to one of these states. Other states have retirement friendly tax policies. For example, South Carolina doesn't tax Social Security income, and it offers seniors a $15,000 deduction on any other type of retirement income, like pensions. Property taxes there are among the lowest nationwide. Research state income and property taxes as part of your retirement planning if you want to relocate.

Will Social Security be there for me?

Republican Mitch McConnell, Majority Leader of the US Senate, once said that members of the Millennial Generation think they have a better chance of seeing a UFO than their Social Security checks. Indeed, the 2016 Transamerica retirement study reveals that

Gen-X (1965 to 1985) is worried too. When asked if Social Security would be there for them in their old age, a staggering 86 percent said they weren't sure it would be.

If the media is to be believed, the future of Social Security is bleak. A large part of the uncertainty is due to gridlock in Congress. Congress did cut benefits in 2015, but it did so very quietly as part of the Bipartisan Budget Act. The point is that tinkering with Social Security, in even a minor way, is viewed as something akin to stepping on the electrified third rail in a subway tunnel. Nobody wants to take a chance, so nothing substantive gets done.

If no real changes are made, the latest statistics indicate that the Social Security program will start to run short of money starting in 2034. At that point, retirees would receive only 77 percent of the benefits they are owed. That's still better than nothing, of course, but more than half of Americans rely on Social Security for 50 percent of their retirement income. It's safe to say that millions of Americans will suffer if Congress continues to kick the can down the road.

Here's one more noteworthy set of numbers. The worker-to-beneficiary ratio was 3.2 to 1 in 1975. It dropped to 2.8 to 1 in 2016. Flash forward to 2040. Estimates suggest that the worker-to-beneficiary ratio will be only 2.1 to 1. That means fewer workers will be paying into the program as Americans continue to age at faster rates. According to AARP, ten thousand Americans turn sixty-five every day!

There are sensible options available to Congress, if it chooses to act. None of them will be painless for the American people, but some are less odious than others. Some options include the following:

Raise payroll taxes
At present, the Social Security payroll tax is 12.4 percent. The self-employed pay the whole thing while employers match half of the payment for their employees. Gradually raising the payroll tax to 14.98 percent would keep the program solvent.

Raise the wage cap
Wages subject to the Social Security payroll tax in 2019 are $132,900. After you reached that number, you no longer had to pay into Social Security. Eliminating or substantially raising the wage cap would greatly bolster the solvency of the program.

Cut Social Security benefits
Changing the formulas used to determine monthly checks, thereby reducing the benefit amounts, would help shore up the Social Security program.

Tax 100 percent of Social Security income
The maximum amount of taxable Social Security income in 2019 s 85 percent. The burden of this option would land mostly on affluent retirees. Retirees with lower incomes would not feel the pinch as much, if at all.

Reduce cost-of-living adjustments
Some sources say that pursuing just this single option would reduce the projected deficit in the Social Security trust fund by 66 percent.

However, inflation is a real concern. At present, the inflation rate is about 2 percent per year. That's still substantial when you consider that FDIC-insured fixed income investments like certificates of deposit pay much less than that. Inflation is not expected to soar like it did in the 1970s during the OPEC oil embargo, at least not any time soon. However, over time, inflation slowly eats away at your purchasing power. Reducing or eliminating COLA is a recipe for disaster for senior citizens.

Raise the full retirement age
We'd see about a 33 percent contribution toward reducing the shortfall if full retirement age was gradually raised from sixty-seven to sixty-nine by 2022. Congress put a similar graduated increase into effect starting with dates of birth in 1955 and going to 1959, whereby you had to add two months to your full retirement age from 1955 to 1959. In 1959, full retirement age had risen to ten months after your birthday in your full retirement year. In 1954, you reached full retirement at sixty-six on your birthday. You reached your full retirement age of sixty-seven on your birthday if you were born in 1960 or later.

The most likely future prognosis for Social Security is that it will not go away, but changes will be made to shore up the program. Our best recommendation for you is not to give in to the temptation to take your retirement benefits early just because you're afraid of future changes. If you're reading this guide, you're very likely in your fifties or early sixties. Any changes that do come will most likely not impact you to any great extent, if at all. If you're from a younger generation, there should be optimism that a sophisticated combination of options can guarantee that Social Security will still play a pivotal role in funding your retirement.

What's the Windfall Elimination Provision?

If you have a government pension from a public service job, including work in foreign countries, that didn't require payment into Social Security, you'll have to have worked in a side or new career that did pay into Social Security in order to qualify for Social Security benefits. You'll need a minimum of forty quarters to qualify. Your Social Security benefits will be reduced by about 50 percent under the Windfall Elimination Provision.

The reasons for the reduction are complicated. Simply put, Social Security benefits are calculated using a progressive formula that favors lower earners. Under the above scenario it would look like you were a low earner because your main job was not reflected in your earnings history used to calculate your Social Security benefits (the highest thirty-five years of earnings). Thus, your Social Security benefits would not accurately reflect the real story. Your Social Security benefits would be reduced to reflect what is fair.

What's a government pension offset?

If you receive a government pension and did not pay into Social Security, but your spouse or ex-spouse did pay into Social Security for more than forty quarters, you might be eligible for spousal benefits. However, two thirds of your pension payments will offset the Social Security payments. The GPO can sometimes wipe out any spousal benefits you may have otherwise received. The GPO is also applied to survivor benefits. The GPO doesn't impact minor or disabled children drawing on your Social Security record.

My spouse receives Social Security retirement benefit checks. What happens when my spouse dies? Do I have to give back the check issued in the month of death?

Social Security pays a month behind, so the check received in the month of death is payable. You wouldn't have to give it back. Notify the Social Security Administration as quickly as possible upon the death of a spouse, if that spouse is drawing Social Security benefits.

CHAPTER 3
Taking Early Benefits

Despite the fact that they know they shouldn't, most Americans take their Social Security retirement benefits at sixty-two. A recent study from the Center for Retirement Research in Boston, Massachusetts, reported that 42 percent of men and 48 percent of women took their benefits as soon as they could. Compare that to the low number of Americans who took benefits at sixty-three and sixty-four—7 percent for men, and 8 percent for women. The numbers increase to 34 percent for men and 27 percent for women between the ages of sixty-five and sixty-six.

The data from the study is revealing. While it does show that the majority of us take reduced Social Security benefits at sixty-two, it also shows that many of us wait until we're either at or near full retirement age before we begin collecting our retirement benefits. Waiting to collect your retirement benefits can greatly increase them.

Let's analyze important questions about taking Social Security retirement benefits early.

Why shouldn't I take my Social Security benefits early?

Claiming your benefits before full retirement age could be a big mistake. Your retirement benefits are reduced for life, and your survivor benefits for a spouse are also reduced. You are eligible for Social Security retirement or spousal benefits starting at age sixty-two.

If you were born before 1954, your full retirement age is sixty-six. If you were born between 1955 and 1959, add two months after your birthday to determine your full retirement age. In other words, if you were born in 1955 you'd add two months to your birthday. If you were born in 1956, you'd add four months to your birthday. If you were born in 1959, your full retirement age would be ten months after your birthday. If you were born in 1960 or later, your full retirement age is sixty-seven.

Waiting to collect your Social Security benefits even one or two years after age sixty-two can pay big dividends. The reduction in benefits is about 6 percent per year between age sixty-two and full retirement age. At sixty-two, your reduction is about 25 percent if you collect as soon as you're eligible and your full retirement age is sixty-six. At sixty-four, the reduction is only about 13 percent, so it makes sense to wait as long as you can before taking your benefits. Ideally, you'll wait until you reach full retirement age, or longer. The chart below breaks the data down for you.

Year of Birth	Full Retirement Age	Percentage of unreduced benefits by year of collection					
		62	63	64	65	66	FRA
1943-1954	66	75%	80%	86.67%	93.33%	100%	100%
1955	66 +2 mo.	74.17%	79.17%	85.56%	95.22%	98.89%	100%
1956	66 +4 mo.	73.33%	78.33%	84.44%	91.11%	97.78%	100%
1957	66 +6 mo.	72.5%	77.5%	83.33%	90%	96.67%	100%
1958	66 +8 mo.	71.67%	76.67%	82.22%	88.89%	95.56%	100%
1959	66 +10 mo.	70.83%	75.83%	81.11%	87.78%	94.44%	100%
1960 and later	67	70%	75%	80%	86.67%	93.3%	100%

Let's put this all in perspective. In the introduction, we said the average individual monthly Social Security check in 2019 is $1,461 or $17,532 per year. If your full retirement age is sixty-six and you wait until then to collect, you'd receive $23,376 if you were an average earner. If you take your benefits at sixty-two, you'll lose 25 percent of that annual benefit for life, or a whopping $5,844 per year! Considering that half of us rely on Social Security for 50 percent of our retirement income you can see that losing benefits by taking them early will take money out of your pocket. In just ten years, the loss would equal $58,440!

Does it ever make sense to take Social Security early?

Health issues can come into play. If you don't think you'll live to age seventy-eight, you lose nothing by taking your benefits early. It takes that long to break even. Bear in mind, though, that life expectancy is increasing all the time. At this point, it's possible to live well into your nineties, and you should plan on that unless you're in very poor health.

It can make sense to collect Social Security early if you need the income for some reason. For example, a job loss with dim prospects for future gainful employment could make taking benefits early a sensible thing to do. Of course, if you have sufficient cash flow from other sources and you don't really need your full retirement benefits from Social Security you can take your benefits early without worrying about the benefit reduction.

Does taking a reduced Social Security benefit early also mean that my spouse's benefits will be reduced?

Taking your retirement benefits early will reduce the amount of survivor benefits for your spouse, but your spouse can still get unreduced spousal benefits on your record by waiting until full retirement age to begin receiving monthly Social Security checks. At full retirement age, your spouse's spousal benefits will be equal to 50 percent of your full retirement benefits. In most cases, spousal benefits will not exceed your retirement benefits. In that instance, you would get your retirement benefits instead of spousal benefits.

If I take spousal benefits early, are they reduced?

Taking Social Security benefits early automatically reduces them. If you wait until full retirement age to collect your spousal benefits, you will receive a monthly check equal to 50 percent of your spouse's full retirement benefits. The same applies if you are an eligible ex-spouse. In other words, your spousal benefits won't be reduced no matter when your spouse takes his or her retirement benefits.

If you take your spousal benefits at sixty-two and your full retirement age is sixty-six, you will only receive about 35 percent of your spouse's retirement benefits, not the full 50 percent you would have received had you waited until your full retirement age to collect spousal benefits. Again, your retirement benefits must be worth less than 50 percent of your spouse's retirement benefits in order for you to qualify for spousal benefits.

The following chart shows your benefit reductions if you take spousal benefits before you reach full retirement age.

Year of Birth	Full Retirement Age	Percentage of unreduced spousal benefits by year of collection					
		62	63	64	65	66	FRA
1943-1954	66	35%	37.5%	41.67%	45.84%	50%	50%
1955	66 +2 mo.	34.59%	37.09%	40.97%	45.14%	49.31%	50%
1956	66 +4 mo.	34.17%	36.67%	40.28%	44.45%	48.61%	50%
1957	66 +6 mo.	33.75%	36.25%	39.59%	43.75%	47.92%	50%
1958	66 +8 mo.	33.24%	35.84%	38.89%	43.06%	47.22%	50%
1959	66 +10 mo.	32.92%	35.42%	38.2%	42.36%	46.53%	50%
1960 and later	67	32.5%	35%	37.5%	41.67%	45.84%	50%

When does it make sense to take my spousal benefits early?

In most cases if you've worked and paid into Social Security for more than the required forty quarters to be eligible for benefits, your retirement benefits will exceed those of your spousal benefits as a current or ex-spouse. In other words, spousal benefits usually don't come into play.

That said, if you have never worked and paid into Social Security, spousal benefits could be a godsend to you as a current or ex-spouse. If your spouse is at full retirement age and is drawing high retirement benefits, you could take spousal benefits at sixty-two. Those benefits could allow you to retire early. Likewise, you could receive survivor benefits if your spouse dies. If you're divorced and you've never worked, taking reduced spousal benefits combined with alimony checks could improve the quality of your life. Since alimony doesn't count against the earnings limit you could even work a job that paid under or just over the earnings limit to add more income to your cash flow. In 2019, the earnings limit was $17,640.

Is it true that if I take Social Security early I won't start losing money for seventeen years?

You will start losing money immediately in terms of a reduced monthly check when you begin receiving benefits before reaching full retirement age. However, there is something known as a break-even point on benefits you took early. When you reach about age seventy-eight, it will have taken that long to receive enough benefits to equal the higher amount you would have received had you waited until you reached full retirement age before you began to collect benefits.

The idea is that if you began taking your retirement benefits at sixty-two and your full retirement age is sixty-six you would have been receiving reduced benefits you wouldn't have had if you'd waited until full retirement age to collect. The monies paid to you during that time add up fast. The majority of Americans take their retirement benefits early, though doing so should only occur after a careful analysis of health, investments, pensions, rental income, and so forth. If you have adequate cash flow to supplement your Social Security, taking benefits early can make sense, especially if you want to retire before your full retirement age.

If we need the income, which spouse should take Social Security benefits early?

Most often the spouse with the lower lifetime earnings should consider taking his or her-Social Security benefits early. The benefits will provide income while the spouse with the higher lifetime earnings delays taking benefits for as long as possible, preferably to age seventy, to maximize benefits through delayed retirement credits.

This is a great strategy in terms of survivor benefits as well. If the higher earning spouse dies, then the survivor benefits for the lower earning spouse will be higher. If the lower earning spouse waits until full retirement age, the survivor benefits will be equal to 100 percent of the higher earning deceased spouse's full retirement benefits. Chances are the survivor benefits will be greater than the retirement benefits of the lower earning spouse.

Does it make sense to use my investments to defer taking my Social Security benefits until age seventy?

If you have investments like a 401(k), traditional IRA, and/or a Roth IRA, drawing these down first to grow your Social Security benefits may be prudent. This is especially true if you want to retire at sixty-two or earlier. The longer you defer taking your benefits, the more they will grow. Distributions from a 401(k) and a traditional IRA are taxed as ordinary income. Distributions from a Roth IRA are not taxed at all, making a Roth IRA a very attractive retirement investment. If you are working with a certified financial planner or wealth manager, he or she will be able to assist you in optimizing your retirement cash flow.

www.ingramcontent.com/pod-product-compliance
Lightning Source LLC
Chambersburg PA
CBHW072254170526
45158CB00003BA/1071